West Africa

Anthony Ham

James Bainbridge, Tim Bewer, Jean-Bernard Carillet, Paul Clammer,
Mary Fitzpatrick, Michael Grosberg, Robert Landon,
Katharina Kane, Matt Phillips

MINDELO (p240)
Lively city with beautiful colonial architecture and a musical soundtrack like no other

CAPE VERDE

Santo Antão
Mindelo
São Vicente
Sal
São Nicolau
Boa Vista

0 — 100 km
0 — 60 miles

Fogo
Mt Fogo (2829m)
Santiago
Maio
PRAIA
Brava

ATLANTIC OCEAN

CHINGUETTI (p565)
Ancient caravan town with all the silent gravitas of the Sahara and surrounded by sand dunes

DAKAR (p683)
West Africa's most cosmopolitan city with terrific beaches, nightlife and Franco-African sophistication

To Cape Verde (445km) (see inset)

THE GAMBIA (p291)
'Africa for beginners' with its traveller-friendly world of beach hammocks and lively markets

ARQUIPÉLAGO DOS BIJAGÓS (p450)
A world away from West Africa's clamour with isolated idyllic beaches and traditional cultures

FREETOWN (p753)
City on the upswing with lively nightlife, good beaches and wildlife-viewing not far away

FOUTA DJALON (p418)
Lush, green world of rolling hills and fascinating mix of cultures still holding fast to tradition

MOROCCO

Laayoune — To Marrakesh
To Oran
Tindouf

Western Sahara Route

Bir Moghrein

Tropic of Cancer

Taghaza

Zouérat
Kediet Ijill (915m)

Taoudenni
El Khnâchich

Nouâdhibou
PN du Banc d'Arguin
Choûm

MAURITANIA

Atâr
Chinguetti

Akjoujt

Tagânt Plateau

Araouane

Sahara

NOUAKCHOTT

Aoukar Depression
Qualâta
Timbuktu (Tombouctou)

Lake Faguibine
Goundam

Rosso
Aleg
Kaédi
Kiffa
Ayoûn el-Atroûs
Néma
Nampala

PN aux Oiseaux du Djoudj
Dagana
Saint-Louis
Louga
Linguère
Matam
Yélimané
Nioro
Nara

PN de la Langue de Barbarie
Diourbel
Réserve de Faune du Ferlo
Kidira
Kayes

DAKAR
Thiès
Kaolack

SENEGAL

Tambacounda
Bafoulabé
PN de la Boucle du Baoulé
Niono
Ségou
Djenné
Mopti
Douentza
Falaise de Bandiagara
Bandiagara
Bankass

THE GAMBIA
BANJUL
Georgetown
PN du Niokolo-Koba
Kédougou
Manantali
Kita
BAMAKO
Koulikoro
Kati
San
Tougan
Yako
Ouahigouya

Ziguinchor
Bafatá
Koupdara
Kéniéba
Kangaba
Sélingué/Dam
Sikasso
Bobo-Dioulasso
Banfora
Gaoua

GUINEA-BISSAU
BISSAU
Gapoul
PN du Bafing
Siguiri
Bougouni
Sindou/Peaks
Diébougou
Batié

Arquipélago dos Bijagós
Jemberem
Boké
Fobané
Fria
Labé
Fouta Djalon
Dinguiraye
Kankan
Manankoro
Korhogo
Ferkessédougou
PN des Deux Balés
Réserve de Bontioli

Bolama-Bijagós Biosphere Reserve
Boffa
Dalaba
PN du Haut Niger
Faranah
Odienné
PN de la Comoé
Bole

CONAKRY
Kindia
Île de Los
Kambia
Kissidougou
Beyla
Séguéla
Bouaké
Aboisso
Techiman

SIERRA LEONE
FREETOWN
Bonthe
Bo
Kenema
Forêt Classée de Ziama
Mt Nimba/Mont Nimba (1752m)
Mont Sanghé
PN du
Man
Ambikéléro
Sunyani

Tiwai Island Wildlife Sanctuary
N'zérékoré
Réserve Intégrale du Mont Nimba
Duékoué
Daloa
YAMOUSSOUKRO
Bia

Robertsport
LIBERIA
Macenta

MONROVIA
Buchanan
Sapo NP
PN de Taï
Soubré
Gagnoa
Agboville
Grand Bassam
Abidjan
Nzulezu

Greenville
Sassandra

Harper

CÔTE D'IVOIRE

GUINEA

MALI

Niger River
Senegal River
Gambia River

VEGETATION

Desert
Semidesert
Grassland
Savanna
Tropical Rainforest

LEGEND

FR   Forest Reserve
GR   Game Reserve
NP   National Park
NR   Nature Reserve
PN   Parc National

Primary
Secondary
Tertiary
Unsealed

0 — 500 km
0 — 300 miles

LIBERIA (p462)
Home to some of West Africa's most optimistic people as the country enjoys its best chance of peace in decades

SASSANDRA (p275)
Fascinating rainforest-fringed fishing village and close to some of Africa's best beaches